The Scopes "Monkey" Trial

Sabrina Crewe and Michael V. Uschan

Gareth Stevens Publishing

A WORLD ALMANAC EDUCATION GROUP COMPANY

Please visit our web site at: www.garethstevens.com
For a free color catalog describing Gareth Stevens Publishing's list of high-quality
books and multimedia programs, call 1-800-542-2595 (USA) or 1-800-387-3178
(Canada). Gareth Stevens Publishing's fax: (414) 332-3567.

Library of Congress Cataloging-in-Publication Data

Crewe, Sabrina.
    The Scopes "Monkey" trial / by Sabrina Crewe and Michael V. Uschan.
      p. cm. — (Events that shaped America)
    Includes bibliographical references and index.
    ISBN 0-8368-3415-1 (lib. bdg.)
    1. Scopes, John Thomas—Trials, litigation, etc.—Juvenile literature. 2. Evolution—
Study and teaching—Law and legislation—Tennessee—Juvenile literature. I. Uschan,
Michael V., 1948-. II. Title. III. Series.
    KF224.S3C74 2005
    345.73'0288—dc22
                                  2004058183

This North American edition first published in 2005 by
Gareth Stevens Publishing
A WRC Media Company
330 West Olive Street, Suite 100
Milwaukee, WI 53212 USA

Produced by Discovery Books
Editor: Sabrina Crewe
Designer and page production: Sabine Beaupré
Photo researcher: Sabrina Crewe
Maps and diagrams: Stefan Chabluk
Gareth Stevens editorial direction: Mark J. Sachner
Gareth Stevens editor: Monica Rausch
Gareth Stevens art direction: Tammy West
Gareth Stevens production: Jessica Morris

Photo credits: Bryan College: pp. 14, 15; Corbis: cover, pp. 5, 6, 7, 8, 9, 11, 12, 17
(right), 18, 20, 21, 22, 23, 24, 25, 27; Eva Cruver: pp. 10, 13, 16, 19, 26; Library
of Congress: p. 4.

Printed in the United States of America

1 2 3 4 5 6 7 8 9 09 08 07 06 05

Contents

Introduction

A Big Trial in a Small Town

For twelve days in July 1925, the attention of the world was focused on a trial taking place in the tiny community of Dayton, Tennessee. On trial was a high school teacher, John T. Scopes. He was charged with breaking a law that banned the teaching of **evolution** in Tennessee schools. Thousands of people came to Dayton to watch the trial, and many more argued hotly about the questions it raised.

This cartoon was published in a newspaper at the time of the Scopes Trial. It shows the effect the trial had on Dayton, Tennessee, when the nation's attention was focused on the town.

EVOLUTION IN TENNESSEE

Important Issues

The questions in the Scopes Trial that stirred the passions of people were these: How did people come to inhabit the world we live in? Did human beings evolve over millions of years from different, "lower" forms of life, as scientist Charles Darwin claimed? Or were they created fully formed by God, in the space of one day, as is written in the Bible?

The trial caused people to talk about the beginning of human life on Earth, but that was not the actual issue on trial. The Scopes Trial's central issue was one of freedom: freedom to speak and worship according to personal belief. The people who defended Scopes's right to teach evolution believed the Tennessee law denied him freedom of speech and gave government approval to one particular religion—Christianity. For those reasons, they said, the law went against the U.S. **Constitution**.

The Outcome of the Trial

The Scopes Trial ended in a dramatic courtroom battle between two famous lawyers, Clarence Darrow and William Jennings Bryan. John Scopes was then found guilty of breaking the law that banned the teaching of evolution. For years afterward, the teaching of evolution was avoided in many U.S. schools. It wasn't until the 1960s that the U.S. **Supreme Court** challenged the anti-evolution laws and addressed the issues of freedom of speech and the place of religion in schools.

Clarence Darrow (left) and William Jennings Bryan (right) chat in the courtroom during the Scopes Trial. Before the trial was over, Bryan and Darrow had a very dramatic and now-famous exchange.

Chapter One

Science and Faith

Changes in Daily Life

The 1920s, when the Scopes Trial took place, were exciting years. Recent advances and inventions—such as the automobile, the telephone, electricity, and the airplane—were creating new ways for people to live.

Not everyone was happy, however, that life was being transformed so swiftly. Many people in this era of great change worried that traditional beliefs and ideas were being left behind or changed. More people than ever before were going to high school and college. As younger men and women began to absorb new ideas from higher education, some of their elders became upset because what was being taught was so different from what they had learned in school.

Creation

"In the beginning, God created the heaven and earth. . . . And God called the dry land earth; and the gathering together of the waters called the seas. . . . And God made two great lights: the greater light to rule the day and the lesser light to rule the night: He made the stars also. . . . God created man in His own image, in the image of God, He created him; male and female He created them."

From the first chapter of Genesis in the Bible

A cartoon published in the 1870s pokes fun at evolution. In the drawing, the man in the middle is showing Charles Darwin that he has insulted a gorilla by claiming humans may be descended from apes.

Evolution Versus the Bible

Perhaps no major idea was more **controversial** than evolution. This **theory** challenged something central to the lives of many people—their belief in God.

In 1859, English scientist Charles Darwin first presented his theory of evolution in his book *On the Origin of Species*. At first, his theory was doubted by other scientists. By the 1920s, however, many educated people believed it was true.

The Theory of Evolution

In *On the Origin of Species* and a later book, *The Descent of Man*, Darwin explained his theory of evolution. He believed all mammals, reptiles, fish, birds, and plants had evolved from simpler life-forms over millions of years. All species, including humans, had gone through physical and mental developments to become what they were. This process was called evolution.

During the Scopes Trial, many fundamentalists came to Dayton to protest against the teaching of evolution. At a street stand, T. T. Martin sold his book, *Hell and the High School*, which warned against "the deadly, soul-destroying poison of Evolution."

Religious Opposition

Christian **fundamentalists** in the United States rejected Darwin's theory. It couldn't be true, they said, because it disagreed with the Bible's explanation of human life. In the Bible, God created the entire Universe—including human beings and all other life-forms—in just six days.

Other Christians felt they could accept Darwin's theory of evolution. Christians who believed in evolution claimed God

Christian Fundamentalism

Christian fundamentalists reject evolution because they believe every word of the Bible is fact. One biblical story, for instance, claims a man named Jonah was swallowed by a fish but that God, several days later, made the fish spit Jonah out of its belly unharmed. Some Christians think that the story was written to illustrate how God could help people. A Christian fundamentalist, however, believes a man by that name really was swallowed by a large fish and survived.

could have allowed humans to go through the evolutionary process described by Darwin. They thought, therefore, that the different ideas of evolution and creation could both be true.

Attacking Evolution

By the early 1920s, there was a strong movement to keep Darwin's theory from being taught in the United States. Among the leaders of this anti-evolution movement was William Jennings Bryan, one of the nation's most famous political figures and greatest public speakers.

In 1925, several state **legislatures** were considering laws to ban the teaching of evolution. In Tennessee, John Washington Butler introduced a law that became known as the Butler Act. He said schools should not teach evolution because it contradicted the Bible, which he claimed was "the foundation upon which our American government is built." The Butler Act became Tennessee law in March 1925.

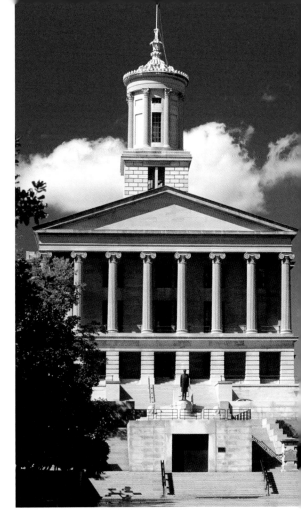

The state capitol in Nashville, Tennessee, as it is today. In 1925, the Tennessee legislature passed the Butler Act in this building.

The Butler Act

"That it shall be unlawful for any teacher in [any] public schools of the State which are supported in whole or in part by the public school funds of the State, to teach any theory that denies the story of the Divine Creation of man taught in the Bible, and to teach instead that man has descended from a lower order of animals."

The Butler Act, passed in Tennessee in 1925

Chapter Two

A Challenge

A large banner outside Robinson's Drug Store in Dayton proclaims its role in the celebrated Scopes Trial.

The ACLU Issues a Challenge

On May 4, 1925, the *Chattanooga Daily Times* printed a story about the American Civil Liberties Union (ACLU). This organization, which supported **civil rights**, had offered to finance a challenge to the recent Butler Act because it believed the new law was **unconstitutional**.

At the Drugstore

Dayton was a small, quiet community in Rhea (pronounced "ray") County, Tennessee, about 40 miles (64 kilometers) northeast of Chattanooga. About 1,800 people lived in Dayton, most of them on farms outside the town.

Like many towns of the period, Dayton had a drugstore with a soda fountain that was a gathering place for the community. A group of businessmen met at Robinson's Drug Store most afternoons to discuss politics, religion, and the town's problems.

The day after the *Chattanooga Daily Times* story came out, the group at the drugstore talked about the ACLU offer. George W. Rappleyea, manager of the Cumberland Coal and Mining Company, was among the few Dayton residents who believed in evolution. One of the people he was talking to was the school superintendent of Rhea County, Walter White, who rejected Darwin's theory.

Hatching a Plot

The two men had argued many times before about evolution. Rappleyea suggested that to settle the issue they should take up the ACLU offer and challenge the Butler Act in court. He pointed out a trial of that kind would attract a lot of publicity, people, and money to Dayton, and that would be good for the town. The idea excited White and the others there: Frank Earle Robinson—the drugstore's owner and chairman of the Rhea County school board—and lawyers Sue Hicks (who was a man) and Wallace C. Haggard.

Some members of the original drugstore group gather for a photograph in Robinson's Drug Store in July 1925. They are (left to right) George Rappleyea, Walter White, Frank Robinson, and Clay Green.

This photo of John Scopes, taken before the trial, shows him reading up on legal matters in a New York law library.

Choosing a Defendant

For the idea to work, the group needed to find a teacher who would go on trial for breaking the anti-evolution law. The biology teacher at Rhea County High School, W. F. Ferguson, refused to take part in the trial. Next, the group sent a message to John Scopes, another teacher at the high school who had taught biology when Ferguson was ill. Scopes came immediately to meet the group at Robinson's Drug Store.

When Rappleyea told him about the group's argument over the Butler Act, Scopes claimed, "I don't see how a teacher can teach biology without teaching evolution."

A Bad Law
"It's a bad law. Let's get rid of it. I will swear out a warrant and have you arrested. That will make a big sensation."

George W. Rappleyea to John T. Scopes, May 5, 1925

The group then asked Scopes to help them challenge the Butler Act by saying he had taught evolution. Scopes agreed to be the **defendant** in the expected trial.

The Charge Is Filed

Rappleyea immediately sent a telegram to the ACLU in New York City, saying that there was going to be a challenge to the Butler Act. The ACLU replied the next day, saying it would provide financial help, legal advice, and publicity.

On May 7, when Rappleyea went to the drugstore again to show the others the reply, they realized they had not yet filed a formal charge against Scopes. Sue Hicks and George Rappleyea wrote out a **warrant** accusing Scopes of teaching evolution. The drugstore group summoned Arthur Benson, a justice of the peace (a local law official), to approve the warrant.

A sheriff then served the warrant on Scopes, who was allowed to remain free. Scopes was formally charged on May 9 in an appearance before three Rhea County justices of the peace, including Benson. He was ordered to stand trial on the charge. The trial was set to start in July 1925.

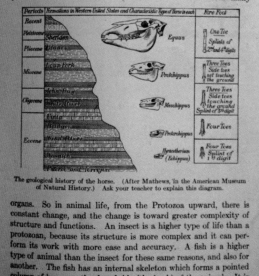

EVOLUTION 193

Increasing Complexity of Structure and of Habits in Plants and Animals. — In our study of biology so far we have attempted to get some notion of the various factors which act upon living things. We have seen how plants and animals interact upon each other. We have learned something about the various physiological processes of plants and animals, and have found them to be in many respects identical. We have found grades of complexity in plants from the one-celled plant, bacterium or pleurococcus, to the complicated flowering plants of considerable size and with many

The geological history of the horse. (After Mathews, in the American Museum of Natural History.) Ask your teacher to explain this diagram.

organs. So in animal life, from the Protozoa upward, there is constant change, and the change is toward greater complexity of structure and functions. An insect is a higher type of life than a protozoan, because its structure is more complex and it can perform its work with more ease and accuracy. A fish is a higher type of animal than the insect for these same reasons, and also for another. The fish has an internal skeleton which forms a pointed column of bones on the *dorsal* side (the back) of the animal. It is a vertebrate animal.

HUNTER, CIV BI. — 17

The biology textbook used at Rhea County High School, Hunter's *Civic Biology*, was used as evidence in the Scopes Trial. This page from the book shows the evolution of a horse.

Chapter Three

The Monkey Trial

Two Dayton girls hold monkey dolls sold during the Scopes Trial.

A Sensational Event

When the Scopes Trial began in July 1925, it appeared as if a giant circus has taken over the normally quiet town of Dayton. Several thousand people and over one hundred reporters came to witness the historic clash. Reporters who wrote or broadcast stories on the Scopes Trial called it the "Monkey Trial," and soon everyone in the nation was talking about what was happening in Dayton.

The streets surrounding the Rhea County Courthouse were jammed with tents set up by traveling preachers, trained chimpanzees riding small bicycles, and vendors selling everything from hot dogs to bibles. As George Rappleyea had hoped, the trial had become a national sensation.

The Lawyers

The **prosecution** and **defense** both assembled teams of lawyers for the case. People were mostly interested in the star attorneys—William Jennings Bryan and Clarence Darrow—because they were two of the most famous men in the United States at the time.

The sixty-five-year-old William Jennings Bryan was a national spokesperson against evolution and a well-known political figure. The defense team's star was the sixty-eight-year-old Clarence Darrow, a lawyer who had been involved in many important trials.

When Bryan came to town, he boldly proclaimed, "The trial between evolution and Christianity is a duel to the death." When Darrow arrived two days later, he told reporters, "John Scopes isn't on trial; civilization is on trial."

Monkey Business

Joe Mendi, a celebrity chimpanzee, was brought to Dayton for the trial.

The "Monkey Trial" name came about because Darwin had stated that human beings shared their ancestry with other primates, an order of mammals that includes monkeys. People on both sides of the issue had fun with the idea that people were related to monkeys. Newspaper cartoons used monkeys to make fun of the trial. Frank Robinson cashed in on the idea by serving a "Monkey Fizz" soda in his drugstore for fifteen cents. Local businesses sold stuffed monkeys and items with the caption "I'm a Monkey's Uncle." Vendors brought in live monkeys dressed in suits and ties, and people paid to have their pictures taken with the animals to prove they had been at the trial.

The Scopes Trial took place in a courtroom on the second floor of the Rhea County Courthouse. The windows of the court-room are on the left in this photograph.

The Trial Begins

The Scopes Trial began on Friday, July 10. More than one thousand people jammed into the small, second-floor courtroom of the Rhea County Courthouse. Outside the courthouse, thousands listened to the trial over loudspeakers. Around the country, others listened in on the radio.

The first day was devoted to **jury** selection. Then, on July 13, the defense team started the trial by arguing that the case

The Butler Act and the Constitution

Darrow believed Tennessee's Butler Act violated the Constitution for several reasons. Under the Fourteenth **Amendment**, states are not allowed to make laws that deny citizens their freedoms and rights as laid out in the Constitution. Two of these rights are free speech and the right to worship in any faith. The law denied Scopes his right to free speech by making it illegal for him to teach an accepted scientific theory. It also denied freedom of worship because it said only the Bible's version of creation was acceptable.

should be dismissed because the Butler Act went against the rules of the U.S. and Tennessee constitutions. Proving the law unconstitutional was the whole point of the trial. Darrow knew the court wouldn't dismiss the case, but that was all right with him. If the court found Scopes guilty, the defense would be able to make an **appeal** to the U.S. Supreme Court. There, Darrow hoped, he could prove the law was unconstitutional and get it overturned.

On July 15, Judge John T. Raulston ruled that the Butler Act did not violate the Constitution. The case would not be dismissed as Darrow had requested.

No Right

"The state of Tennessee, under an honest and fair interpretation of the Constitution, has no more right to teach the Bible as the divine book than that the Koran is one or the book of Mormons or the essays of Emerson or any one of ten thousand books to which human souls have gone for consolation and aid in their troubles."

Clarence Darrow, July 13, 1925

Four-year-old Tommy Brewer (above left) chose possible jurors by pulling names out of a hat. The selected jurors (above right) gathered for a photograph before the trial began. Standing right of the jurors is John Raulston, the trial's judge.

William Jennings Bryan sits at the trial in his under-shirt. The courtroom was so hot that Judge Raulston broke the usual rules and let participants take off their jackets and ties.

No Experts Wanted

"The Bible, the record of the Son of God, the Savior of the world [is] not going to be driven out of this court by experts who have come hundreds of miles to testify that they can reconcile evolution with its ancestor in the jungle."

*William Jennings Bryan,
July 16, 1925*

Prosecution Witnesses

The prosecution then began calling **witnesses** to **testify**. First, Rhea County school superintendent Walter White declared that Scopes admitted he had taught evolution. Next, two students from classes Scopes had taught testified that Scopes had told them about the theory of evolution.

Defense Witnesses

After lunch on July 15, the defense called the first in a series of experts to talk about science and religion. Dr. Maynard Metcalf was a nationally known zoologist and leader in the Congregational Church. He testified that of all the scientists in the United States, "I know there is not a single one among them that doubts the fact of evolution."

The next day, Darrow started questioning Metcalf again. The prosecution suddenly objected, however, saying that testimony about evolution from experts had no bearing on the case and should not, therefore, be permitted. The trial came to a halt.

Raulston Rules

After much arguing between defense and prosecution, Judge Raulston ruled on July 17 that he would not allow

expert witnesses to testify because science and religion were "not the issue" in the trial. Raulston said the only matter that had to be decided was whether Scopes had taught evolution in violation of the Butler Act.

The Courtroom Moves

On Monday July 20, the judge made another announcement. The weight of the huge crowds gathered in the courtroom had caused cracks in the first-floor ceiling below the courtroom. Raulston was afraid the floor could collapse, and the heat in the courtroom was becoming too much anyway. The judge announced he was moving the trial outside.

Everyone moved onto the courthouse lawn. The court officials, judge, attorneys, and defendant sat on a platform usually used by ministers to deliver sermons. Spectators and journalists gathered around the platform on wooden benches, in nearby cars, or on the grass.

A Surprise Witness

As the trial began again, Darrow amazed everyone by asking Bryan to testify. He said he wanted a Bible expert to explain why the theory of evolution was false. The result was a dramatic confrontation.

Biblical Truth

In his testimony, Bryan claimed that "everything in the Bible should be accepted as given there." Darrow asked if that

Clarence Darrow (1857–1938)

Clarence Darrow was born in Ohio and became a lawyer at twenty-one years of age. By the time of the Scopes Trial, he was famous because he had handled so many big cases. Several cases had involved the rights of working people, while others were sensational murder trials. Darrow was a declared agnostic, a person who neither believes nor disbelieves in the existence of a god. Throughout his life, he remained a defender of free thought and free speech.

Clarence Darrow during the Scopes Trial.

A view of the trial during Darrow's questioning shows Bryan, seated on the left, cooling himself with a fan. Darrow is standing center right.

meant Bryan believed a fish really swallowed Jonah and that Jonah emerged from the fish unharmed three days later. Bryan said he did.

The Length of a Day

Darrow later asked Bryan, "Do you think the Earth was made in six days?" Bryan amazed everyone by answering, "Not six days of twenty-four hours." An astonished Darrow asked, "Doesn't it [the Bible] say so?" to which Bryan said, "No sir."

Bryan said a biblical day might have lasted "millions of years." The answer shocked many in the crowd who believed that every word in the Bible was absolutely true, and so a "day" in biblical terms had to be an actual day. Even worse, the answer implied that creation could have lasted long enough to allow for Charles Darwin's theory of evolution.

Days or Periods

Darrow: "Do you think [days in the Bible] were literal days?"
Bryan: "My impression is they were periods."
Darrow: "Have you any idea of the length of the periods?"
Bryan: "No. I don't." . . .
Darrow: "If you call those periods, they may have been a very long time?"
Bryan: "They might have been."
Darrow: "The Creation might have been going on for a very long time."
Bryan: "It might have continued for millions of years."

Testimony of William Jennings Bryan, July 20, 1925

A huge crowd assembled on the courthouse lawn to witness Darrow's fierce questioning of Bryan.

The Trial Is Stopped

After more questions, Bryan finally snapped in anger. He stood up, shook his fist in the air, and accused Darrow of trying to "slur the Bible." Darrow roared back that he was only trying to show Bryan believed in "fool ideas that no intelligent Christian on Earth believes."

William Jennings Bryan (1860–1925)

William Jennings Bryan was born in Salem, Illinois. After becoming a lawyer in 1883, he began a political career. Bryan was famed for his kindness and compassion as well as his public speaking. He was a great supporter of poor working people, especially farmers, and he campaigned for many reforms that would help workers. Later in life, Bryan devoted himself to moral and religious causes, such as opposing evolution. A devout Christian and a **pacifist**, he saw the teaching of evolution as a threat to society.

Almost everyone on the courthouse lawn began shouting and arguing with each other. Fearing a riot, Raulston stopped the trial until 9:00 A.M. the next day.

The Verdict

On July 21, the two sides summed up their cases for the jury. At the end of his summary, Darrow did something no defense lawyer is supposed to do: He asked that Scopes be found guilty. He did that because he wanted to appeal the guilty **verdict** in the Supreme Court and have the Butler Act ruled unconstitutional.

At 11:14 A.M., the jurors left the courtroom to begin considering the case. Just eight or nine minutes later, they returned with a guilty verdict. Scopes made a brief statement, the first words he had spoken at the trial. Judge Raulston then fined him $100, and the trial was over.

An Unjust Statute
"Your honor, I feel that I have been convicted of violating an unjust statute. I will continue in the future as I have in the past, to oppose this law in any way I can. Any other action would be in violation of my ideal of academic freedom —that is, to teach the truth as guaranteed in our Constitution."

John T. Scopes, July 21, 1925

The jury only took a few minutes to return a verdict. This photo shows Scopes (left) with defense lawyer Dudley Field Malone listening to the jury's verdict.

Chapter Four

After the Trial

The Appeal Fails

In January 1926, the defense team from the Scopes Trial made an appeal to the Tennessee Supreme Court. The appeal failed, however, because of a mistake made in the original trial. At the end of the trial, Judge Raulston had set the fine at $100, even though Tennessee law stated that any fines greater than $50 had to be set by the jury. Because of this mistake, the Tennessee Supreme Court reversed the guilty verdict. Without a guilty verdict against John Scopes, the case could not be appealed, and the defense never had the chance to prove the Butler Act was unconstitutional.

Shunning Evolution

In the two years after the trial, Mississippi and Arkansas passed anti-evolution laws similar to Tennessee's. Many textbook publishers deleted material on evolution because they feared school districts would not buy their science books.

A group of students sits at school desks in the 1940s. From the 1920s to the 1960s, many U.S. public schools avoided the teaching of evolution.

For many years, some teachers would not teach Darwin's theory even if their states did allow it. They feared trouble with parents or school boards if they told students about evolution.

An Appeal to the U.S. Supreme Court

In 1964, Susan Epperson, a biology teacher at Little Rock Central High School,

appealed to the U.S. Supreme Court about a 1927 Arkansas anti-evolution law. On November 12, 1968, in the case *Epperson v. Arkansas*, the Supreme Court ruled that the Arkansas law contradicted the First Amendment of the Constitution. The ruling meant that states were no longer allowed to have laws banning the teaching of evolution.

Because of Supreme Court rulings, students in public schools today are entitled to learn about evolution and other scientific theories.

The Stars of the Trial

After the Scopes Trial, William Jennings Bryan remained in Dayton, writing articles and making speeches about the case. On July 26, 1925, just a few days after the trial ended, Bryan took a nap from which he never awoke—while sleeping, he suffered a stroke and died. Clarence Darrow went on to defend a few more cases before he retired from the law to become a writer and lecturer. He died in 1938. After the trial, John Scopes studied geology and then worked for over thirty years as an oil and gas engineer. He died in 1970.

Conclusion

In the Rhea County Courthouse, the courtroom where the Scopes Trial took place has been preserved as it was in the 1920s. The courtroom is pictured here in 2003.

Important Freedoms

"The basic freedoms of speech, religion, academic freedom to teach, and to think for oneself defended at Dayton are not so distantly removed; each generation, each person must defend these freedoms or risk losing them forever."

John T. Scopes, Center of the Storm: Memoirs of John T. Scopes, *1967*

Dayton Today

Robinson's Drug Store in Dayton is long gone. Visitors to the town today, however, can tour the Rhea County Courthouse, now a national historic landmark. In the second-floor courtroom where the Scopes Trial was held, they can sit in chairs used by the trial's participants and view displays about the famous trial.

Residents of Dayton are proud of their past. *Inherit the Wind*, a 1955 play based on the trial, has been performed at the courthouse several times. Together with Bryan College—a Christian college that opened in Dayton in 1930 as a memorial to William Jennings Bryan—the town holds a four-day Scopes Trial Festival every year.

The Debate Continues

The Scopes Trial reflected a great clash in American society between religious tradition and scientific progress. The debate continues today, especially in the continuing conflict over the teaching of evolution and the place of religion in schools.

Christian fundamentalists argue that evolution is only a theory, and it should not be presented to students as proven fact. They say that **creationism** should be taught in schools as an alternative theory to balance the teachings. Creationism, however, gives only the Christian Bible's version of creation, not those of other faiths. In addition, the Supreme Court has ruled that it is not the job of public schools to teach religion.

The Constitution and the Bill of Rights—the first ten amendments—are kept in the National Archives building in Washington, D.C. The First Amendment says that every person has the right to free speech and the right to choose his or her own religion.

Schools, Religion, and the Constitution

The First Amendment of the Constitution says: "Congress shall make no law respecting an establishment of religion, or prohibiting the free exercise thereof; . . ." This clause means that the government, which runs public schools, must not involve itself with religion and must not interfere with people's right to practice their religions. This is what people mean when they talk about separation of church and state.

Time Line

| 1859 | *On the Origin of Species* by Charles Darwin is published. |
| 1925 | March 21: Butler Act is signed into law in Tennessee. |

1859   *On the Origin of Species* by Charles Darwin is published.

1925   March 21: Butler Act is signed into law in Tennessee.

May 5: John T. Scopes agrees to help challenge the Butler Act.

May 7: Warrant is issued against John T. Scopes.

July 10: Scopes Trial begins in Dayton, Tennessee.

July 13: Clarence Darrow argues that the Butler Act is unconstitutional and asks for the case to be dismissed.

July 15: Judge John T. Raulston declares the Butler Act constitutional, and the trial continues.

July 16: William Jennings Bryan argues against allowing the defense to have scientific and religious experts testify on evolution.

July 17: Raulston forbids defense's expert witnesses to testify.

July 20: Darrow calls Bryan to testify as a Bible expert.

July 21: The jury finds Scopes guilty, and Judge Raulston fines him $100.

July 26: Bryan dies in Dayton.

1926   January: Scopes Trial defense team makes an appeal to Tennessee Supreme Court.

1927   January 17: Tennessee Supreme Court reverses Scopes's conviction.

1930   September: Bryan College, named for William Jennings Bryan, opens in Dayton.

1968   In the case *Epperson v. Arkansas*, the U.S. Supreme Court overturns an Arkansas ban on teaching evolution.

Things to Think About and Do

At the Trial
Imagine you were in Dayton, Tennessee, during the time of Scopes Trial. Write about the event, describing the town, the crowds and excitement, and the trial itself.

Inherit the Wind
The play and movie *Inherit the Wind* were based on the story of the Scopes Trial, and the movie is still available on video and DVD today. Watch the movie, and think about how it differs from what you know about the actual events from reading this book. What was changed for the movie? Do you think the movie favors one side rather than the other?

Creation and Evolution
Find out what you can about creation stories from different cultures and faiths in the United States and around the world. How do they fit in with your own beliefs? How do they fit in with the theory of evolution? Do you believe in one creation story more than any other? Why?

Glossary

amendment:	addition to the original U.S. Constitution.
appeal:	request to a higher court to examine and overturn a trial verdict.
civil rights:	basic rights—such as freedom, education, freedom of speech, or choice of religion—of every person.
constitution:	basic rules of government for a nation.
controversial:	causing a lot of discussion and disagreement.
creationism:	belief in the biblical version of creation as a scientific fact.
defendant:	person charged with a crime.
defense:	legal representatives who speak in favor of a defendant.
evolution:	process of change in living things over a long period of time.
fundamentalist:	person who believes strongly in following the basic rules of a religion and in a strict interpretation of religious writings.
jury:	panel of twelve people who decide whether a defendant is guilty or innocent.
legislature:	group of officials that makes laws.
pacifist:	person who opposes war even if his or her country is attacked.
prosecution:	legal representatives who present a case in court against a defendant to prove that he or she is guilty.
Supreme Court:	highest court in the United States or in each state. The U.S. Supreme Court has the power to interpret the U.S. Constitution.
testify:	speak at a trial after swearing to tell the truth. What people say when they testify is called their testimony.
theology:	study of religion.
theory:	explanation of why things happen or are a certain way.
unconstitutional:	going against the U.S. Constitution.
verdict:	decision made by a jury in a trial.
warrant:	document authorizing an arrest or other official action.
witness:	person who gives testimony about something that happened.

Further Information

Books

Graves, Renee. *The Scopes Trial* (Cornerstones of Freedom). Children's Press, 2003.

Webster, Stephen. *The Kingfisher Book of Evolution*. Larousse Kingfisher Chambers, 2000.

Zeitlin, Steve. *The Four Corners of the Sky: Creation Stories and Cosmologies from Around the World*. Henry Holt, 2000.

Web Sites

www.bryan.edu/scopes Bryan College Web site has articles about and photographs of the Scopes Trial.

www.law.umkc.edu/faculty/projects/ftrials/scopes/scopes.htm University of Missouri Famous Trials Web site is a wonderful resource for information on the Scopes Trial and more than thirty other famous trials.

www.pbs.org/wgbh/amex/monkeytrial/ Public television Web site with information, photographs, and audio and video links having to do with the Scopes Trial.

Useful Addresses

Rhea County Courthouse and Scopes Trial Museum
1475 Market Street
Dayton, TN 37321
Telephone: (423) 775-7801

American Civil Liberties Union
125 Broad Street, 18th Floor
New York, NY 10004
Telephone: (212) 549-2500

Index